AC/DC

STIFF UPPER LIP

Art Direction + Design: Alli
Statue Concept + Photography: Mista Dean Karr
Photo Producer: Yamani Y. Watkins
Statue Sculpted by: SMG Effects - Mark Alfrey, Stan Lok
Digital Retouching: Eric Altenburger

Project Editor: Ed Lozano
Transcriptions for publication: Bob Grant,
Hemme B. Luttjeboer, Robert Mangano, Matt Scharfglass

Order No. AM 965668
US International Standard Book Number: 0.8256.1799.5
UK International Standard Book Number: 0.7119.8323.2

Exclusive Distributors:
Music Sales Corporation
257 Park Avenue South, New York, NY 10010 USA
Music Sales Limited
8/9 Frith Street, London W1V 5TZ England
Music Sales Pty. Limited
120 Rothschild Street, Rosebery, Sydney, NSW 2018, Australia

Printed in the United States of America by
Vicks Lithograph and Printing Corporation

CONTENTS

Legend of Music Symbols

Stiff Upper Lip
By Angus Young and Malcolm Young

10

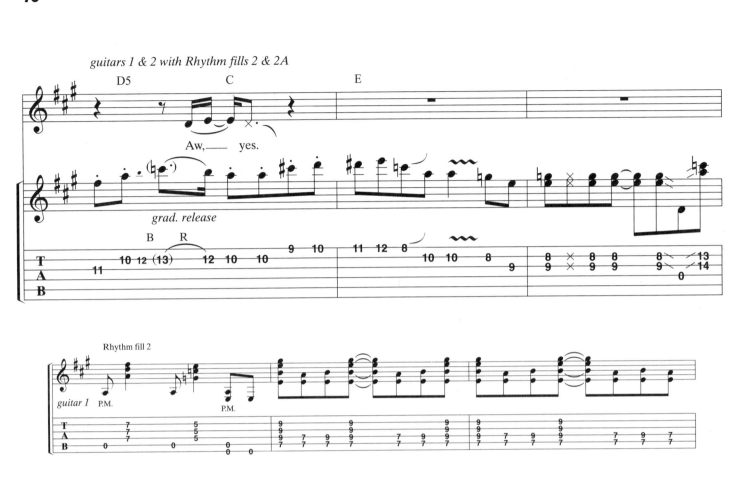

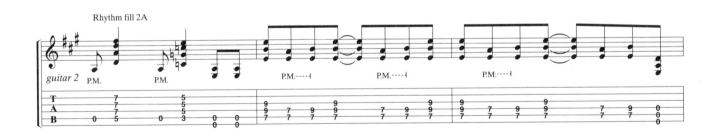

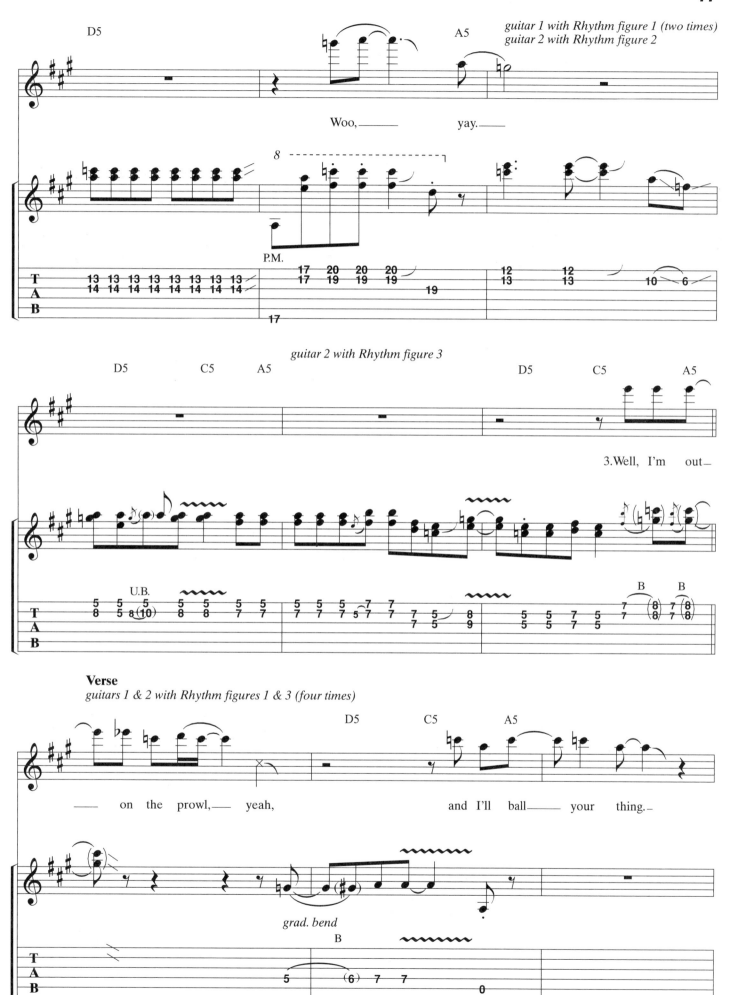

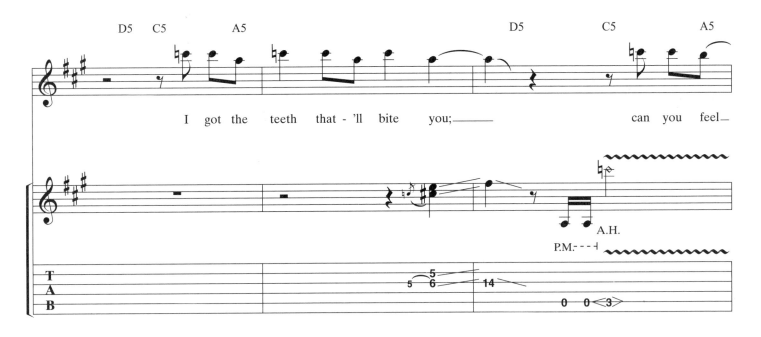

I got the teeth that - 'll bite you;____ can you feel____

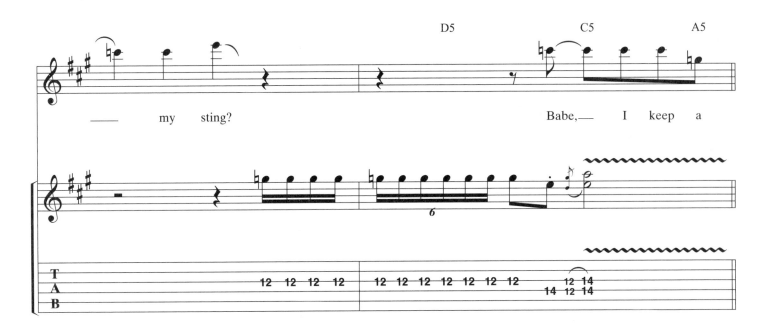

____ my sting? Babe,____ I keep a

Chorus

guitars 1 & 2 with Rhythm figures 1 & 3 (two and a half times)
guitar 3 tacet

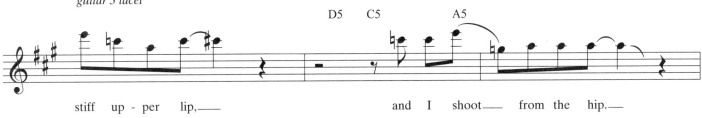

stiff up - per lip,____ and I shoot____ from the hip.

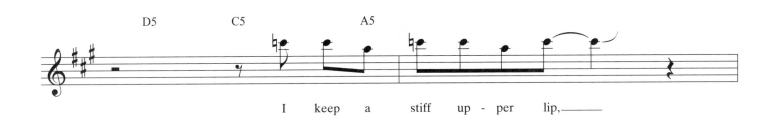

I keep a stiff up - per lip,____

Chorus
with Vocal figure 1 (four times)
guitar 1 with Rhythm figure 1
(four times)
guitar 2 tacet

and I shoot, shoot, shoot from the hip.— I got a stiff.

Bet-ter be-lieve— me, stiff. Com-in' down.

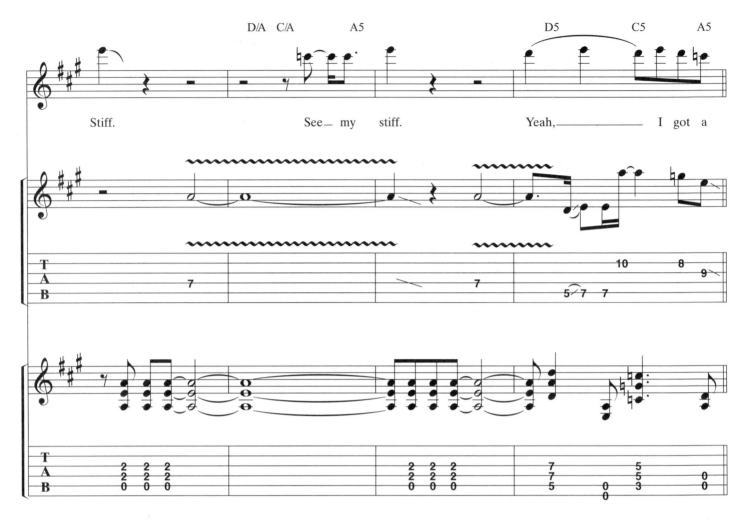

Outro Chorus
with Vocal figure 1 (seven times)
guitar 1 with Rhythm figure 1 (seven times)
guitar 2 with Rhythm figure 2

guitar 2 with Rhythm figure 3 (six times)

Vocal figure 1

shoot from the hip.—

rake ----

*Rapidly flick pickup switch
back and forth.

Additional lyrics

2. Well, I'm workin' it out
   And I've done everything.
   And I can't reform, no;
   Can you fell my sting?
   Man, I keep a...
   (to Chorus)

House of Jazz

By Angus Young and Malcolm Young

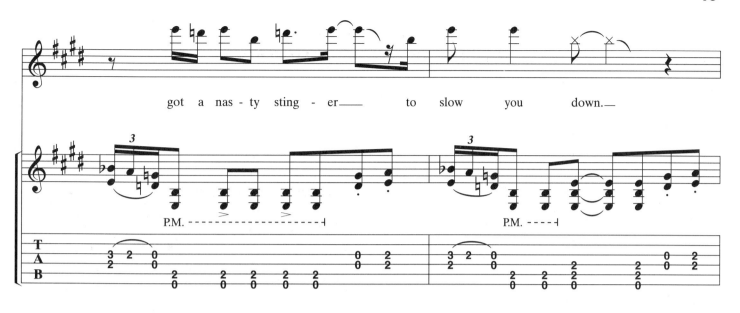

got a nas - ty sting - er___ to slow you down.___

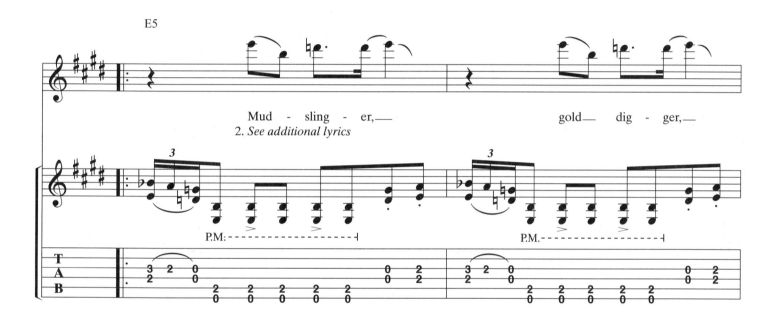

E5

Mud - sling - er,___ gold___ dig - ger,___
2. *See additional lyrics*

who point_ the fin - ger___ and do you down?___

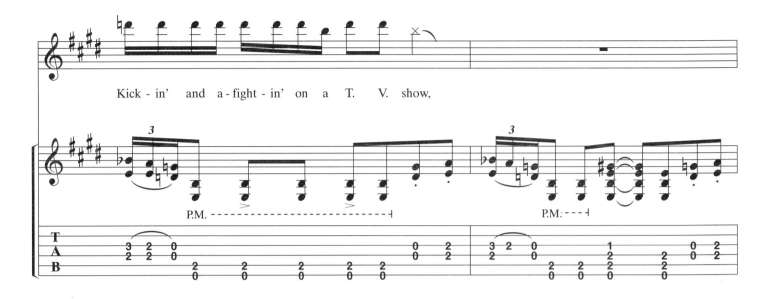

Kick - in' and a - fight - in' on a T. V. show,

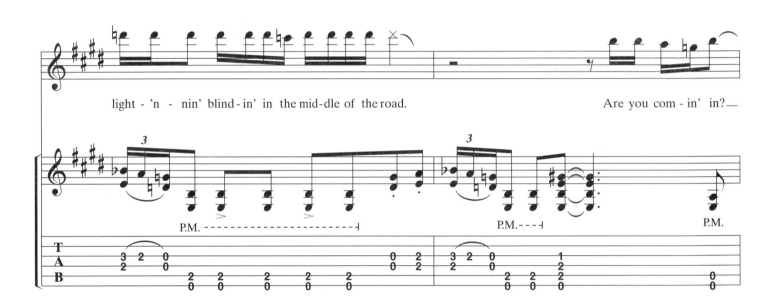

light - 'n - nin' blind - in' in the mid - dle of the road. Are you com - in' in? —

Are you com - in' in? I said...

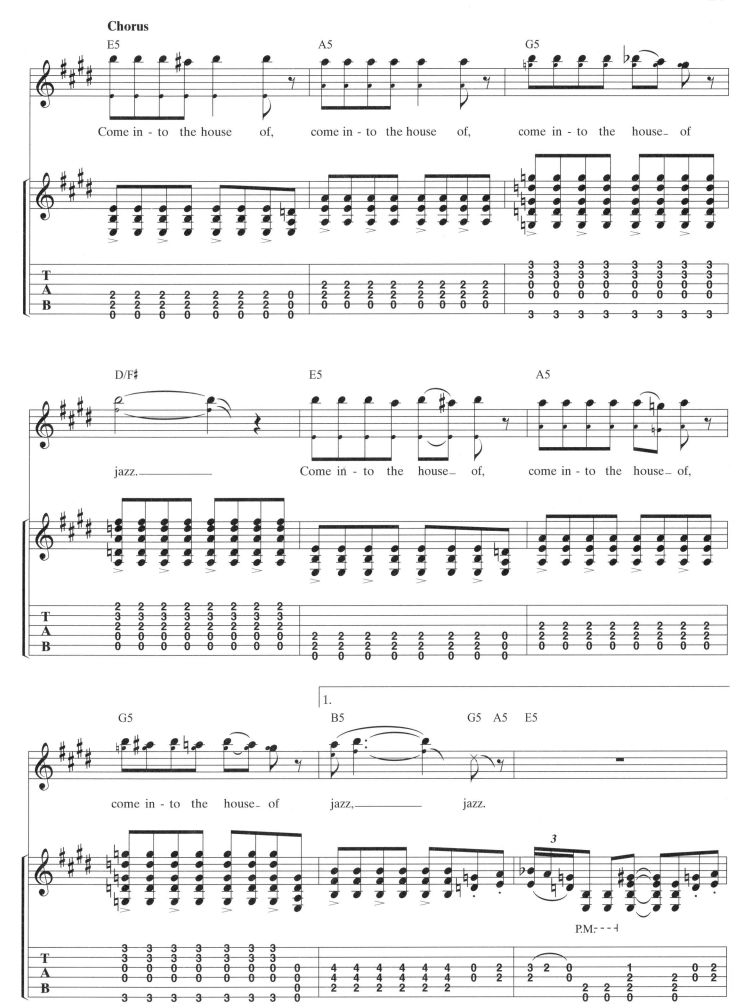

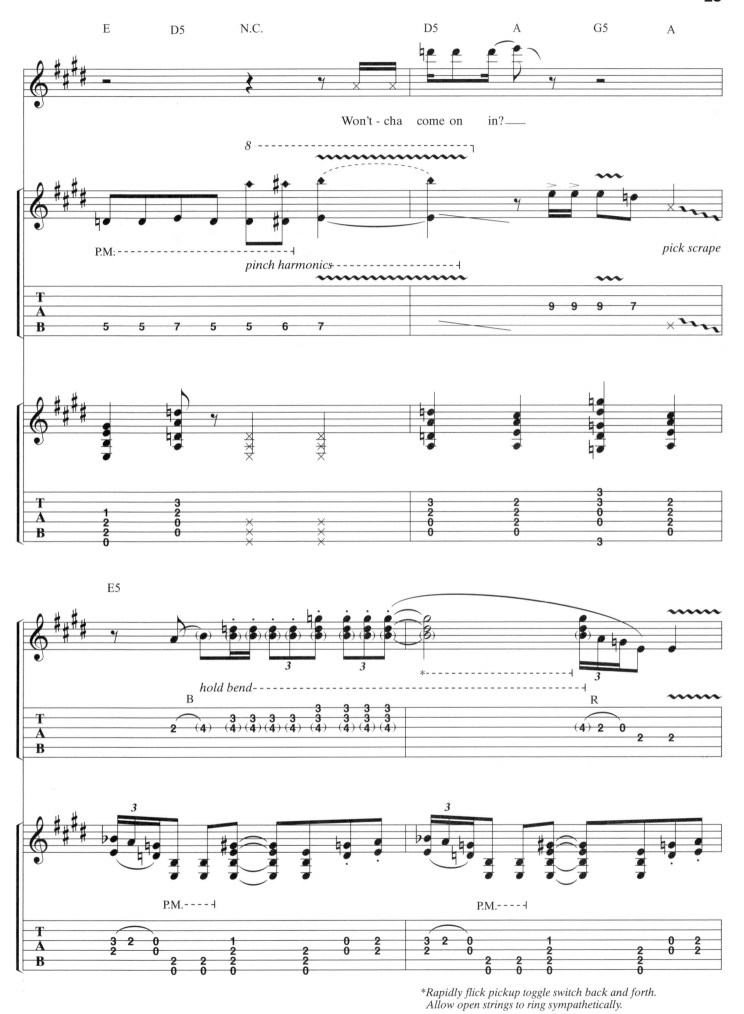

Won't - cha   come on   in? ____

*Rapidly flick pickup toggle switch back and forth.
Allow open strings to ring sympathetically.*

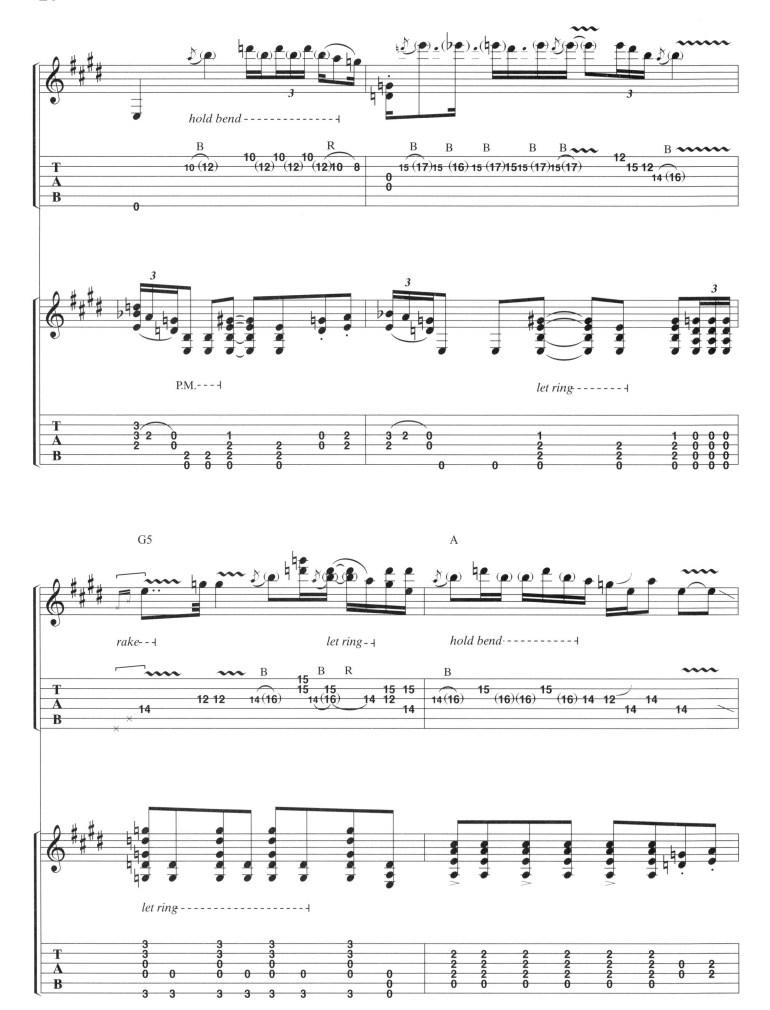

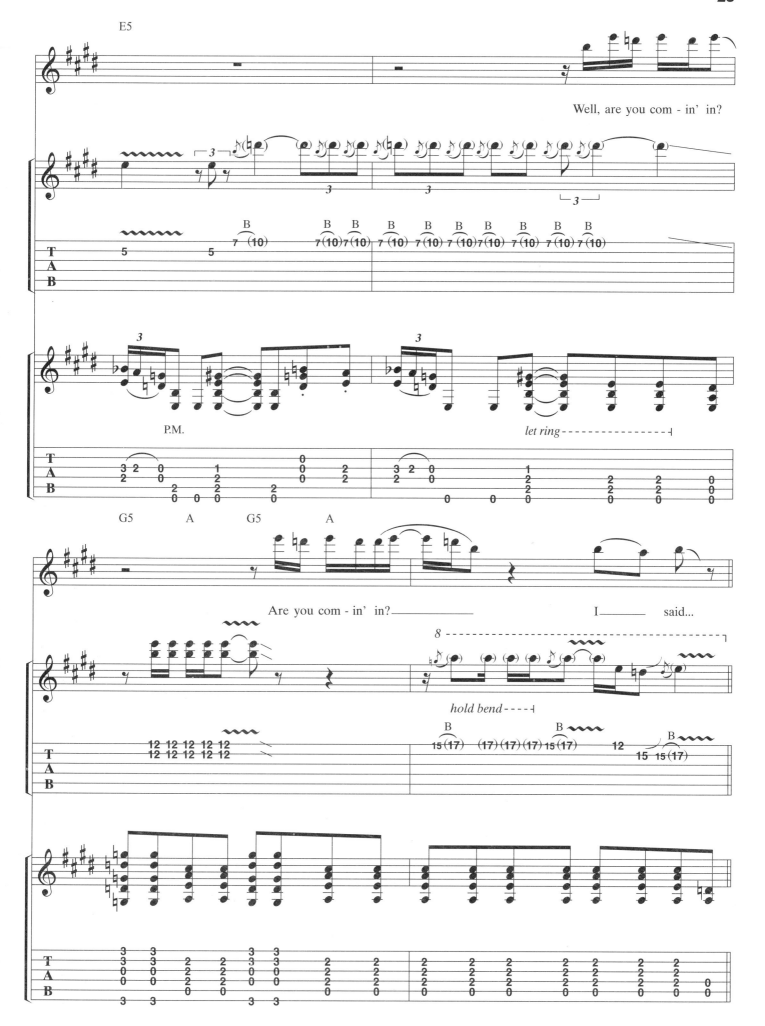

Chorus

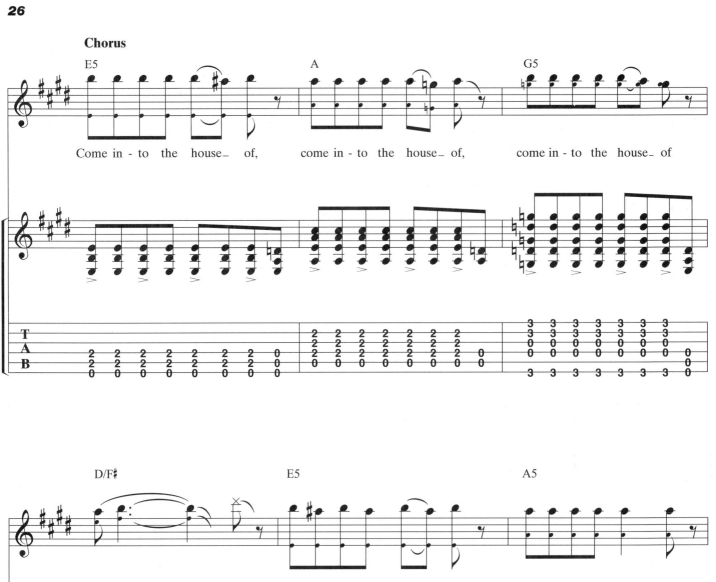

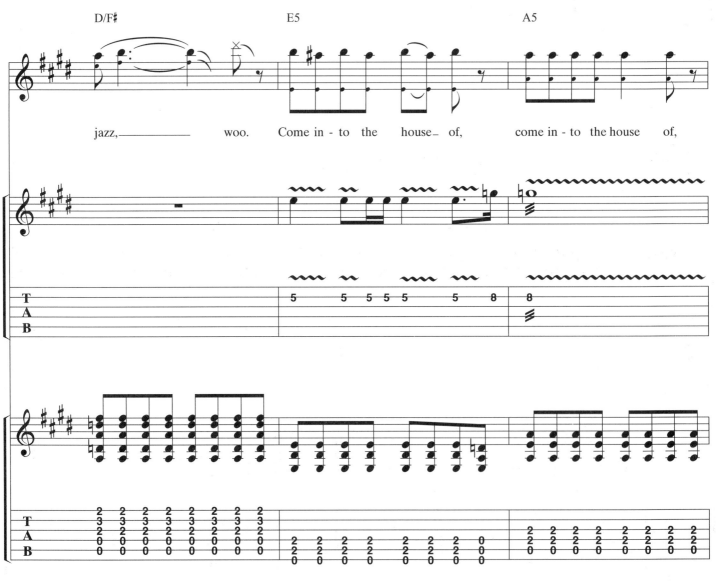

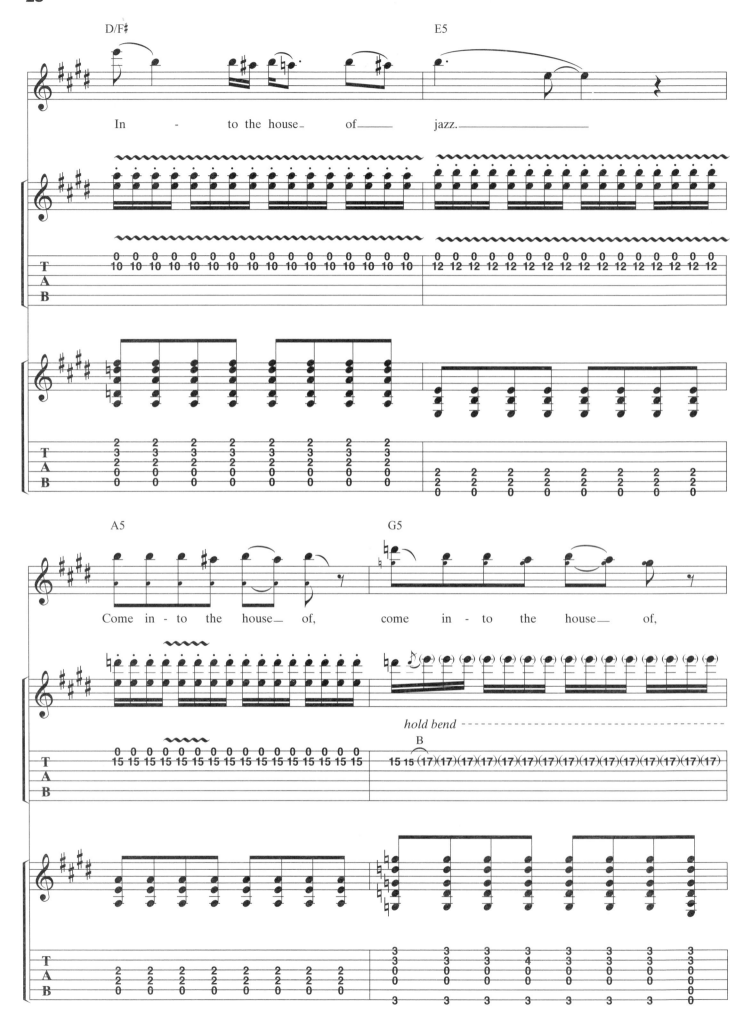

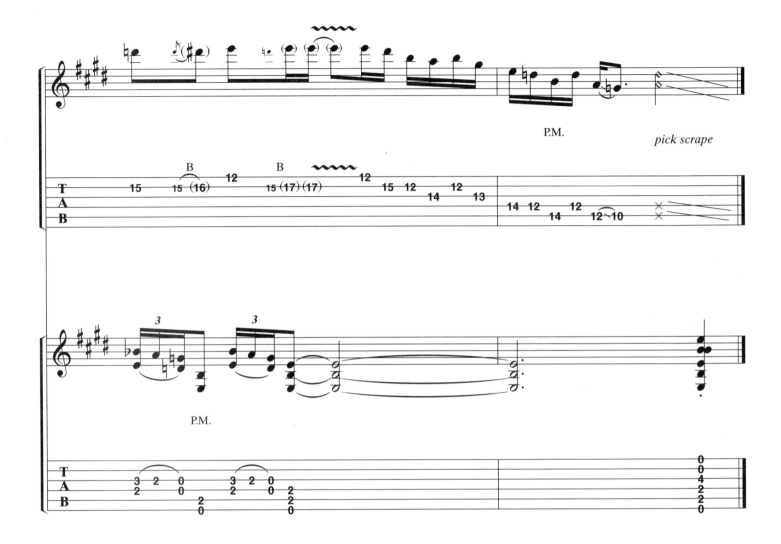

Additional lyrics

2. Ball stripper, big tipper,
   Got a slap and tickler to make you growl.
   A-spittin' and a bitin' on a T.V. show,
   Tightenin', frightenin', givin' out a load.
   Are you comin' in?
   Are you comin' in? I said...
   (to Chorus)

Meltdown

By Angus Young and Malcolm Young

*all downstrokes

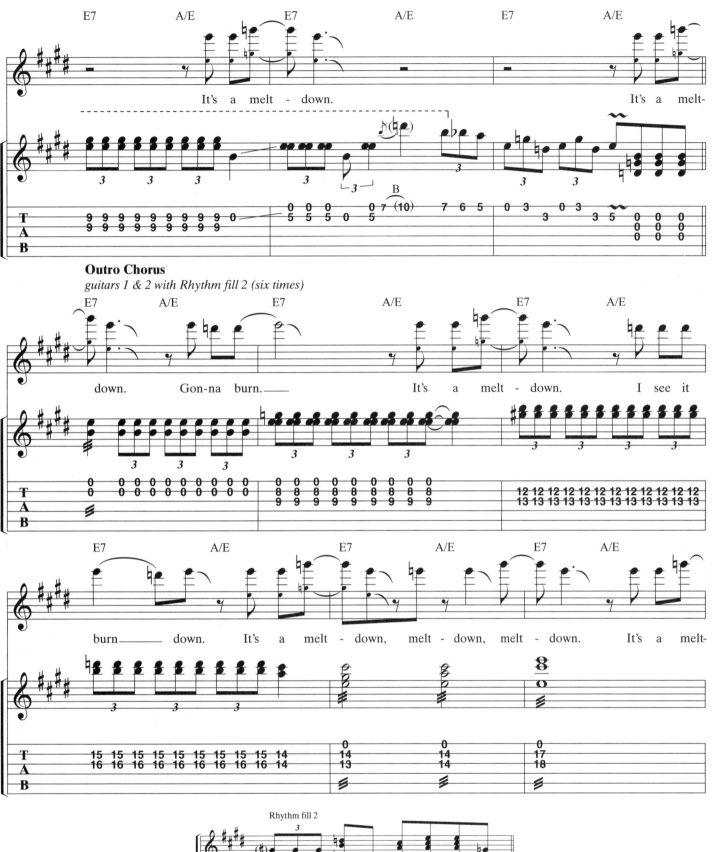

Outro Chorus
guitars 1 & 2 with Rhythm fill 2 (six times)

guitar 1 & 2

two guitars arranged for one.

down.

guitars 1 & 2

guitar 3

all downstrokes (next four measure)

It's a melt - down.

Slower

E

ritard. -

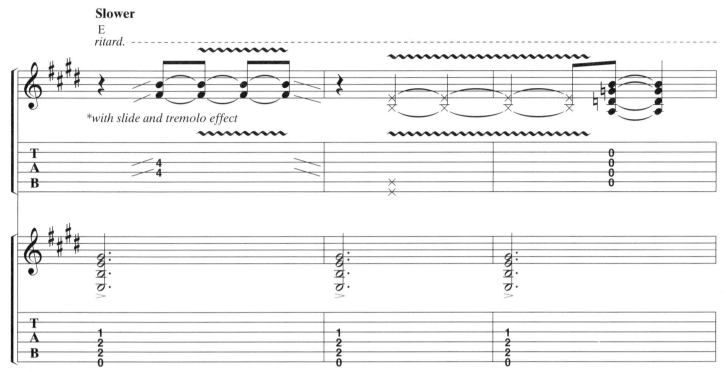

*with slide and tremolo effect

*guitar 3: this part is meant to be played as random, improvised slide and string noise. All pitches and rhythms are approximate.

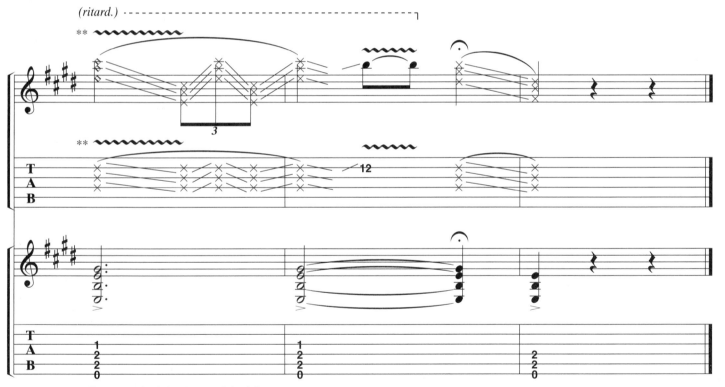

**Execute wide slide vibrato while sliding.

Additional lyrics

2. I got a feelin' in my bones;
   I been rackin' my brains out all night long.
   Stokin' up the fire, take it right up to the wire
   Burnin' on and on, burnin' on.
   (to Pre-Chorus)

Hold Me Back

By Angus Young and Malcolm Young

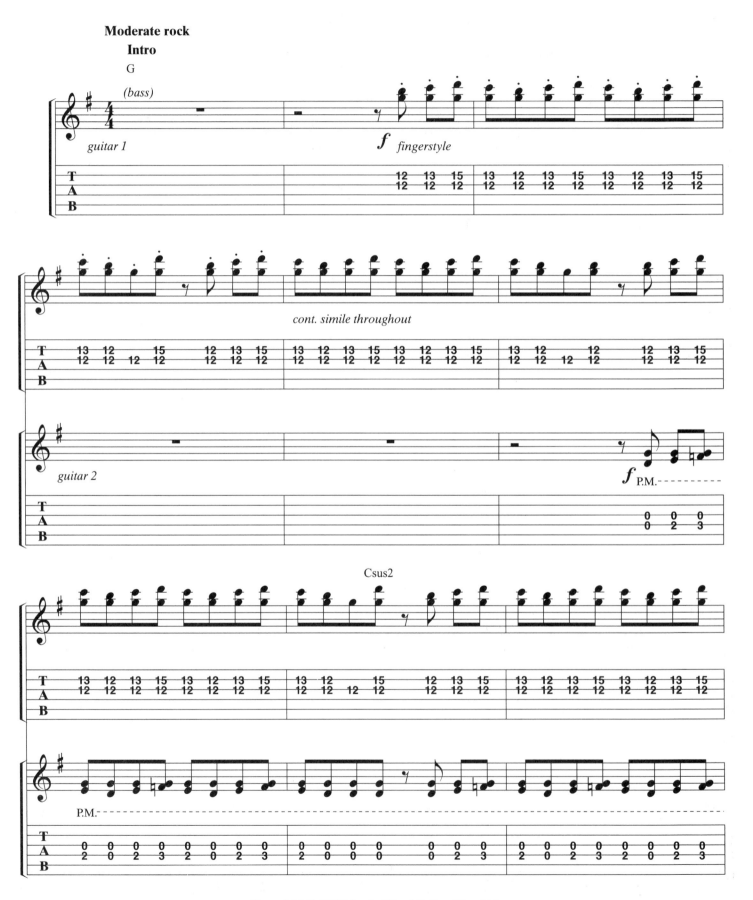

Verse
guitars 1 & 2 play Rhythm figures 1 & 1A on repeat

Chorus

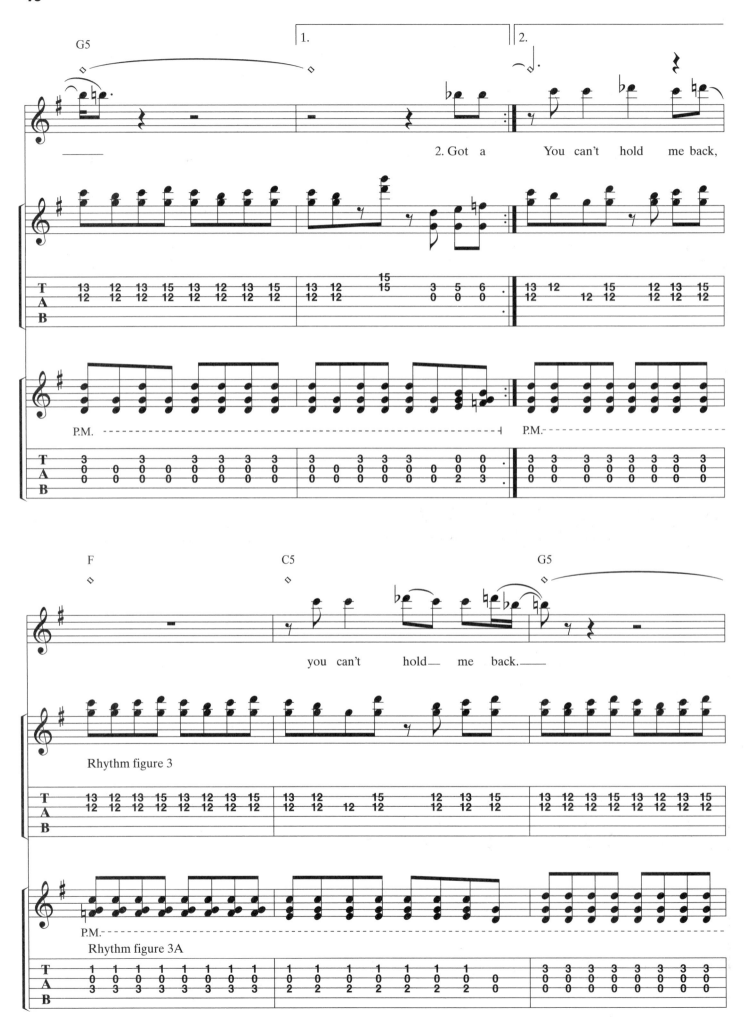

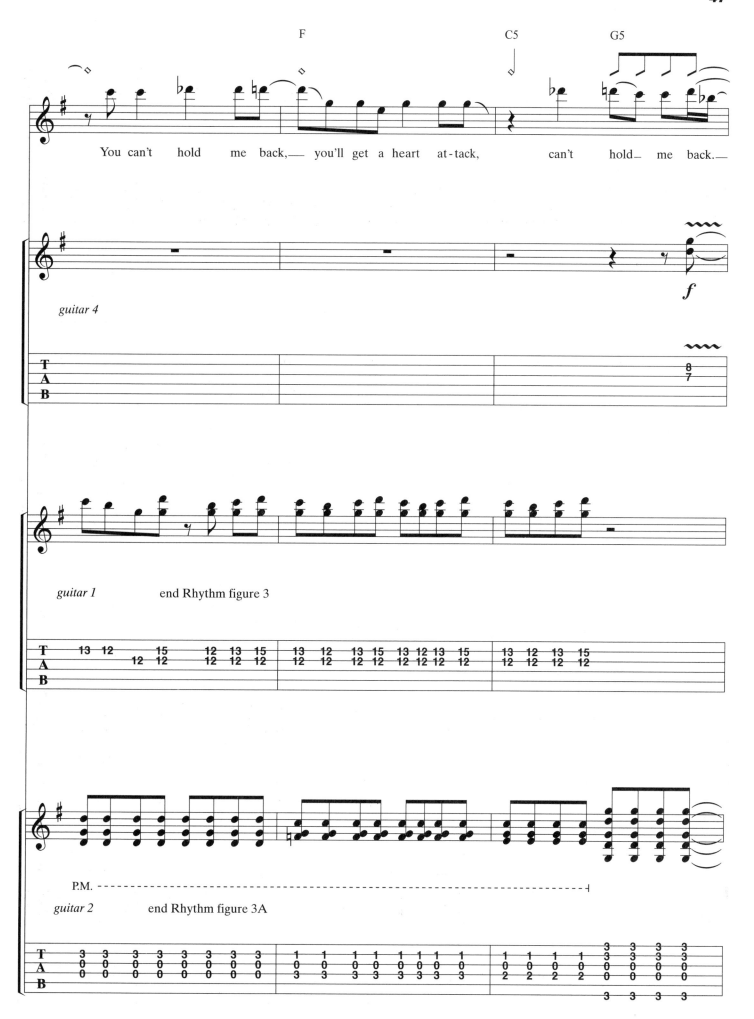

You can't hold me back,— you'll get a heart at-tack, can't hold— me back.—

48

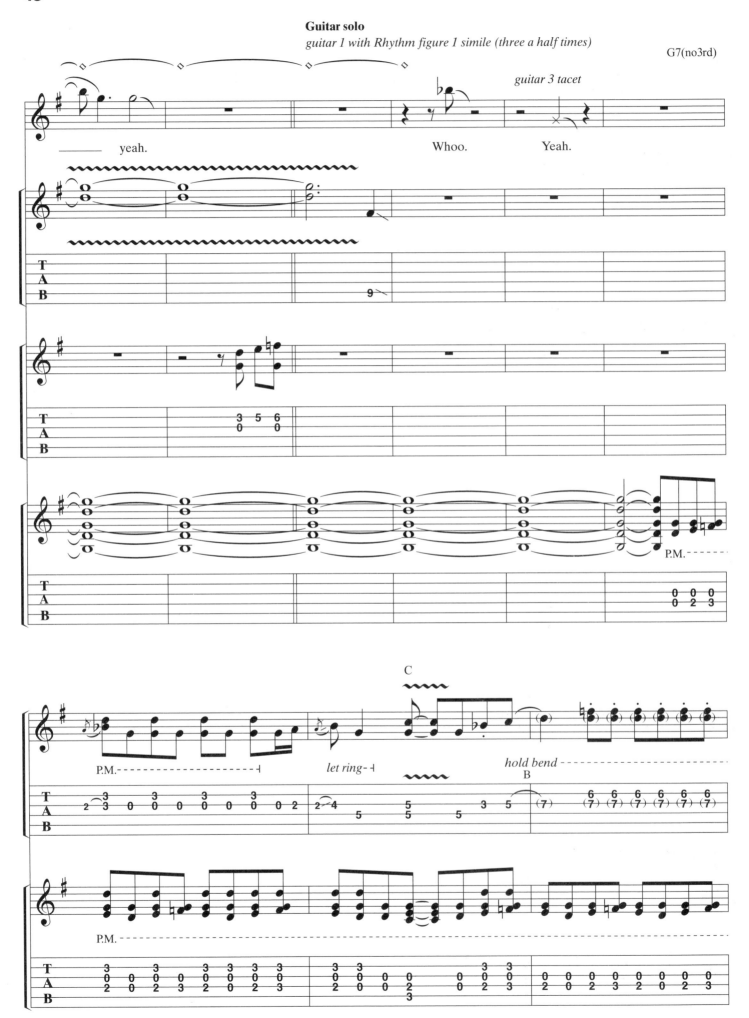

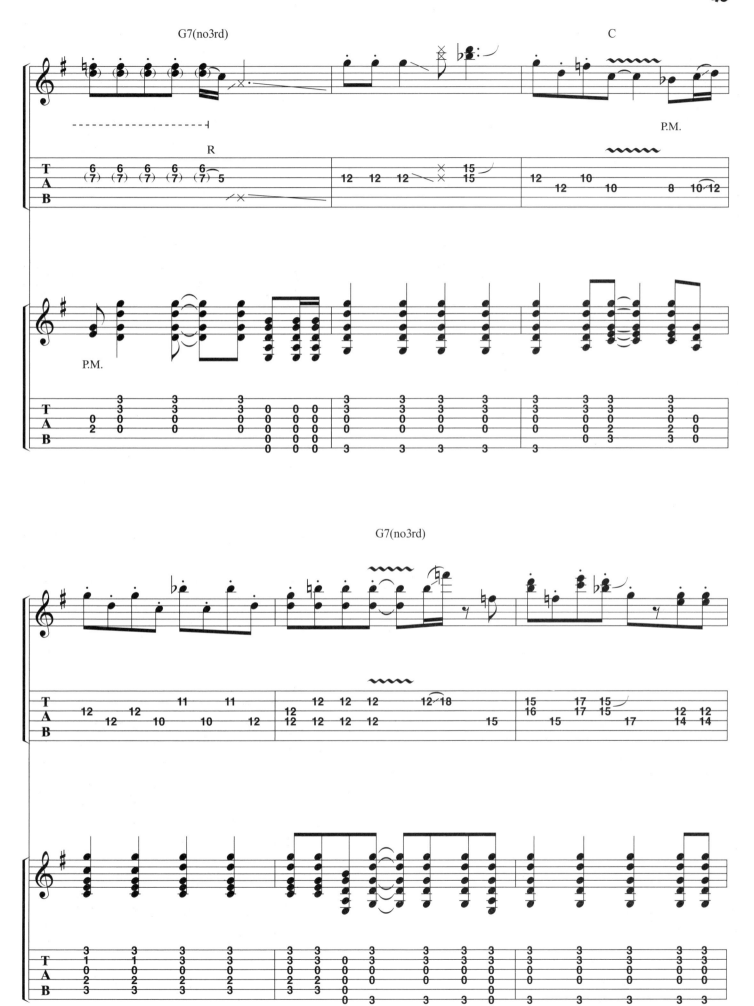

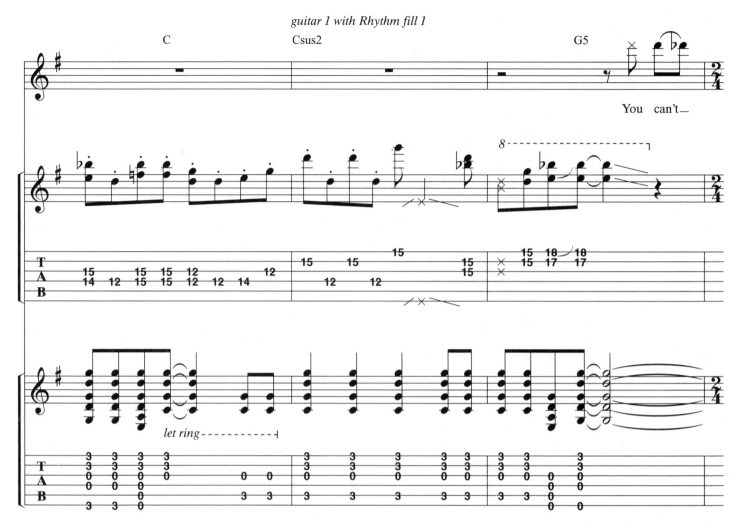

Chorus

guitar 1 with Rhythm figure 2A
guitars 2 & 3 with Rhythm figures 3A and 2 (three and a half times)
guitar 4 tacet

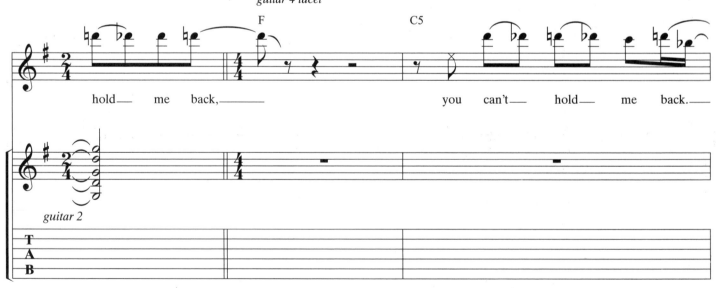

guitar 1 with Rhythm figure 3 (two times)

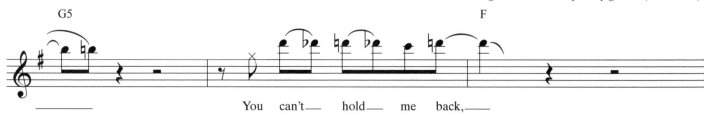

Outro

with Vocal figure 1 (three and a half times)
guitar 1 with Rhythm figure 1 simile (three and a half times)

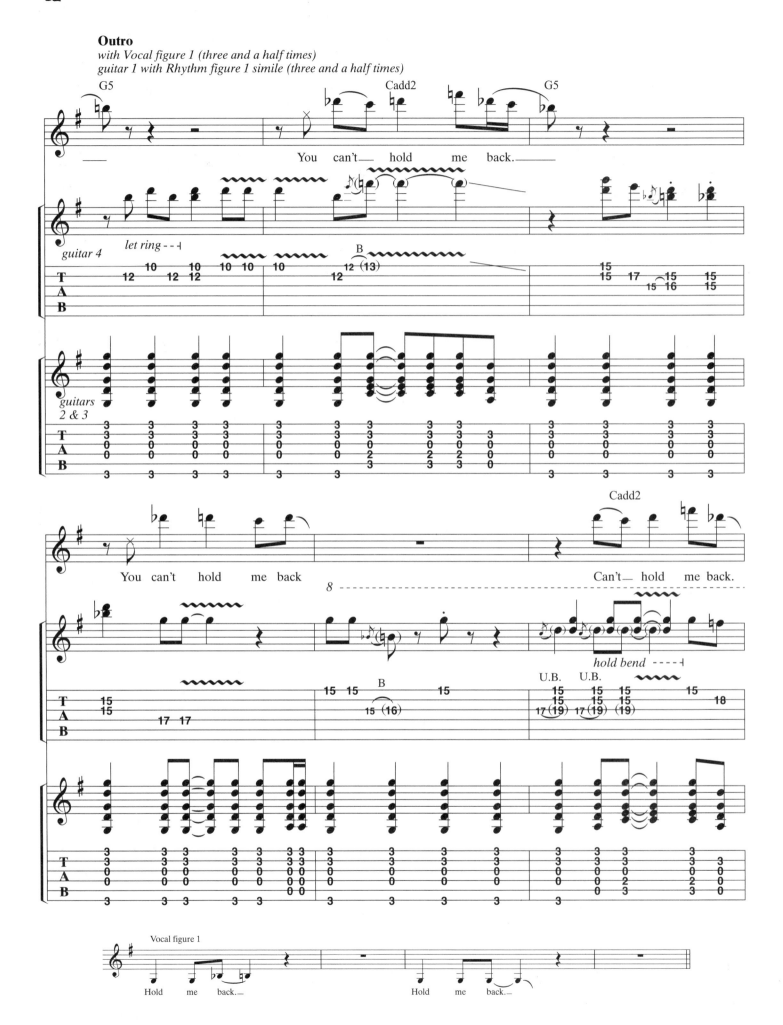

You can't hold me back.

You can't hold me back

Can't hold me back.

Vocal figure 1

Hold me back.

Hold me back.

You can't hold— me back.————

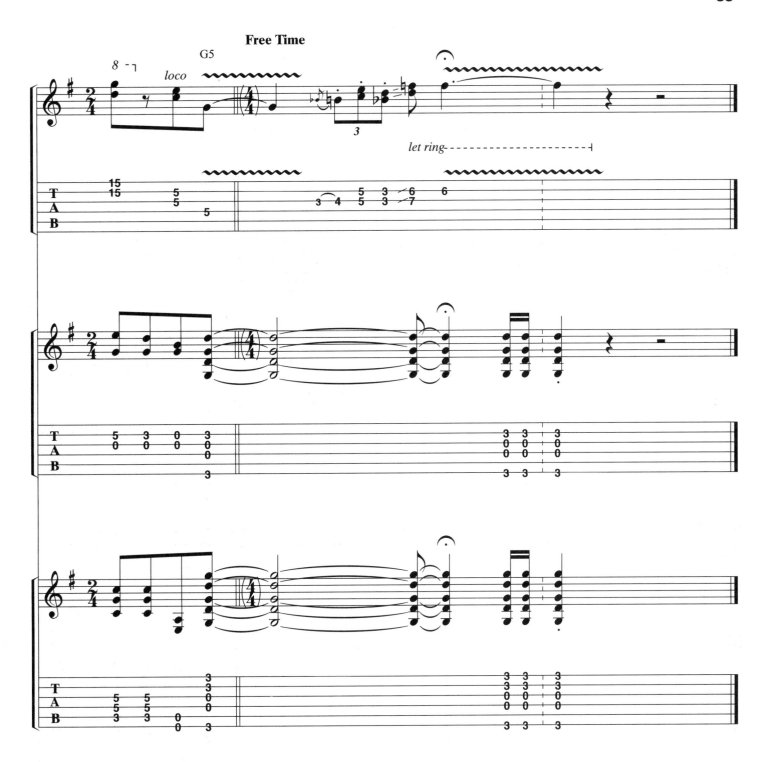

Additional lyrics

2. Got a honky tonk big ball hit to thrill,
   I got a sugar boot money baby that'll kill.
   A honky dog fifteen golden mile,
   Got a bald headed woman loaded in the town
   You can get me to the ball man, drivin' in
   And don't balk the kill, call in the 'ville.
   You gotta map the wrong town, hit the road;
   You got the whole boppa movin' on down the road.
   (to Chorus)

Safe in New York City

By Angus Young and Malcolm Young

*Bass plays E through all verses and choruses.

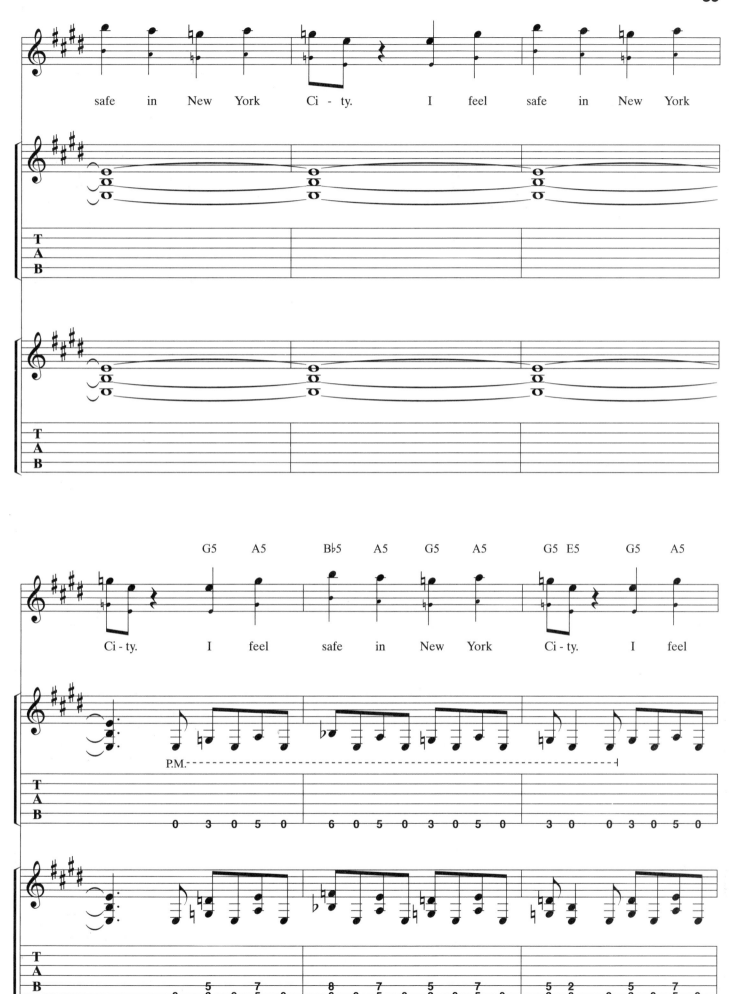

Chorus
guitar 1 with Rhythm figure 2
guitar 2 with Rhythm figure 2A

guitars 1 & 2 with Rhythm fill 1

don't_ you fret,— boy, she's rea-dy to buck.—   I feel

safe— in New York Ci-ty.   I feel safe— in New York

Ci-ty.   I feel safe in New York Ci-ty.   I feel—

Guitar solo II

safe— in— New York Ci-ty.

guitar 3

Rhythm fill 1

guitars 1 & 2

Outro
guitar 2 with Rhythm figure 4A (three times)

*Strike only the bottom note.

**guitars 1 & 2

** two hearts beating as one

*Flick pickup switch back & forth as quickly as possible, gradually slowing
down as bent note is released.*

Additional lyrics

2. All over the city and down to the dives,
  Don't mess with this place, it'll eat you alive, yeah:
  Got a lip smackin' honey to soak up the jam;
  On top of the world ma ready to slam.
  (to Chorus)

Can't Stand Still

By Angus Young and Malcolm Young

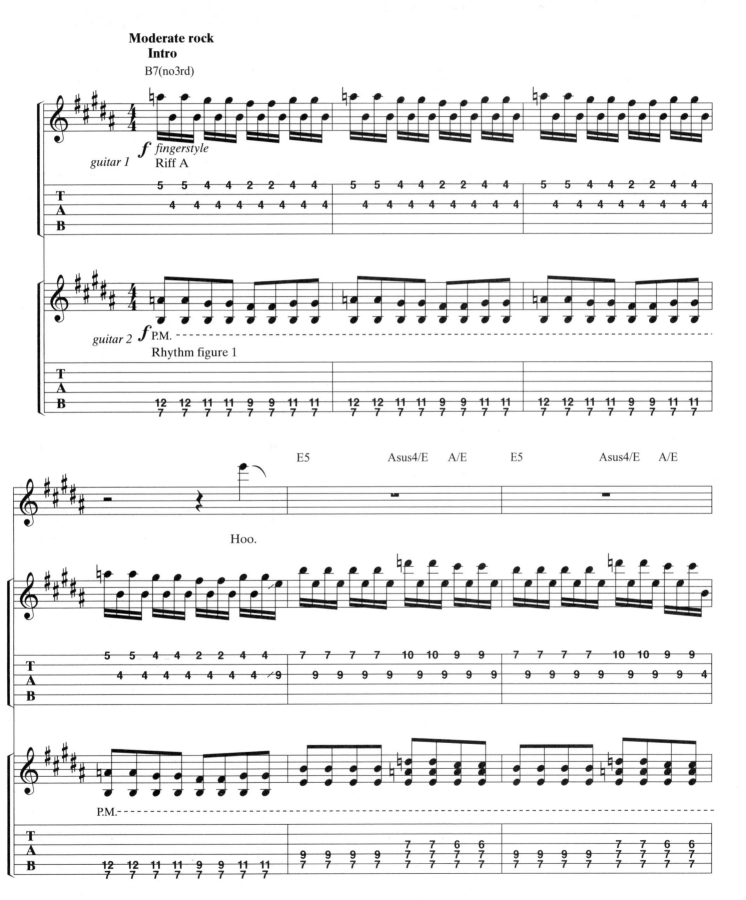

Verse
guitar 1 with Riff A (two times)
*guitar 2 with Rhythm figure 1 (two times)**

B7(no3rd)

see a pret-ty wom - an, you know it give me a thrill.
hear a noi-sy par - ty, you know it give me a chill.

*guitar 2: partially ease up on palm mute during 2nd verse.

3. Well, when it

Outro Chorus
guitar 1 with Riff A (first nine measures)
guitar 2 with Rhythm figure 2 (first nine measures)

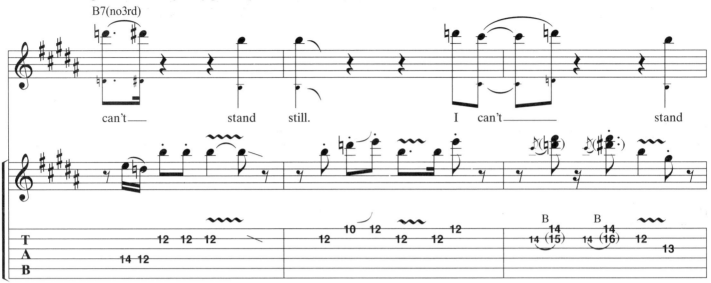

can't___ stand still. I can't_____ stand

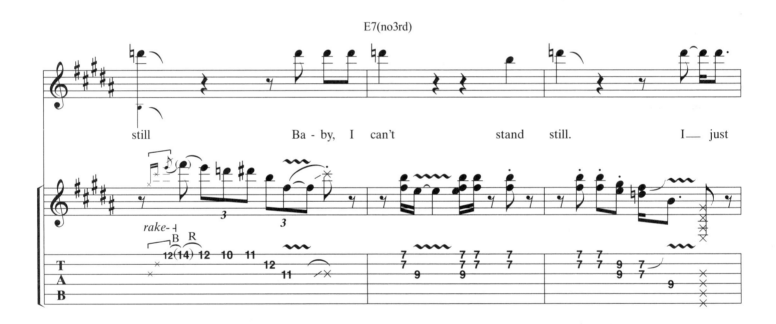

still Ba - by, I can't stand still. I___ just

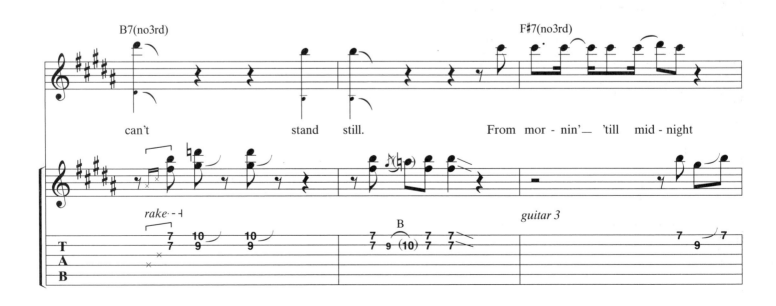

can't stand still. From mor - nin'___ 'till mid - night

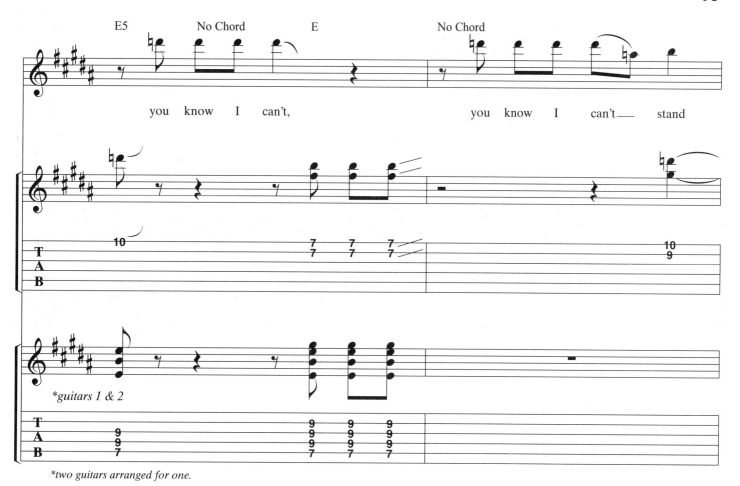

*two guitars arranged for one.

Can't Stop Rock 'n' Roll

By Angus Young and Malcolm Young

1. Don't ya give me no line
2. Don't ya play me no jive

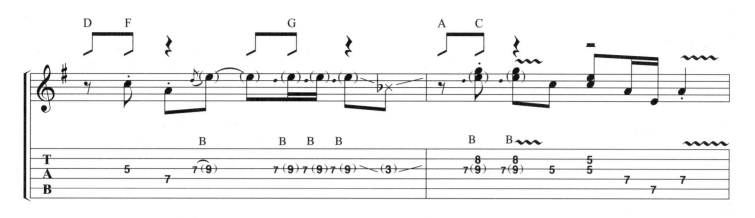

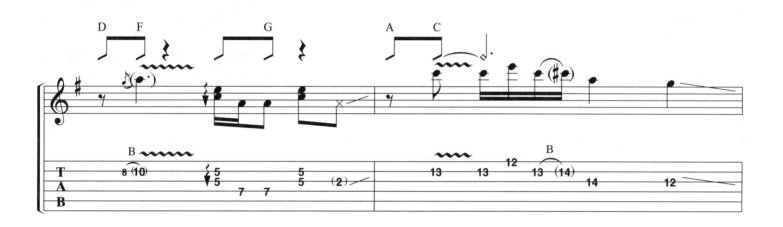

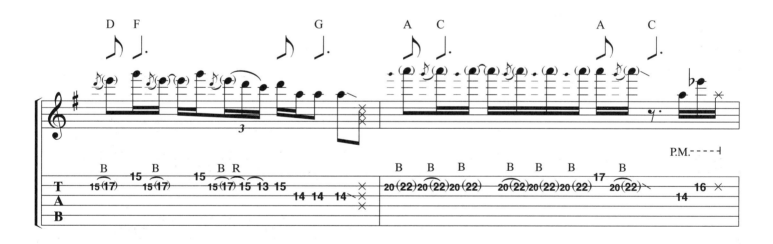

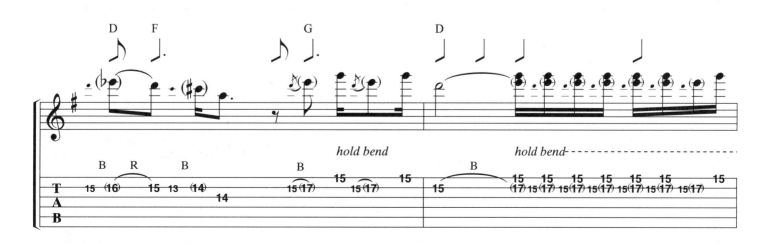

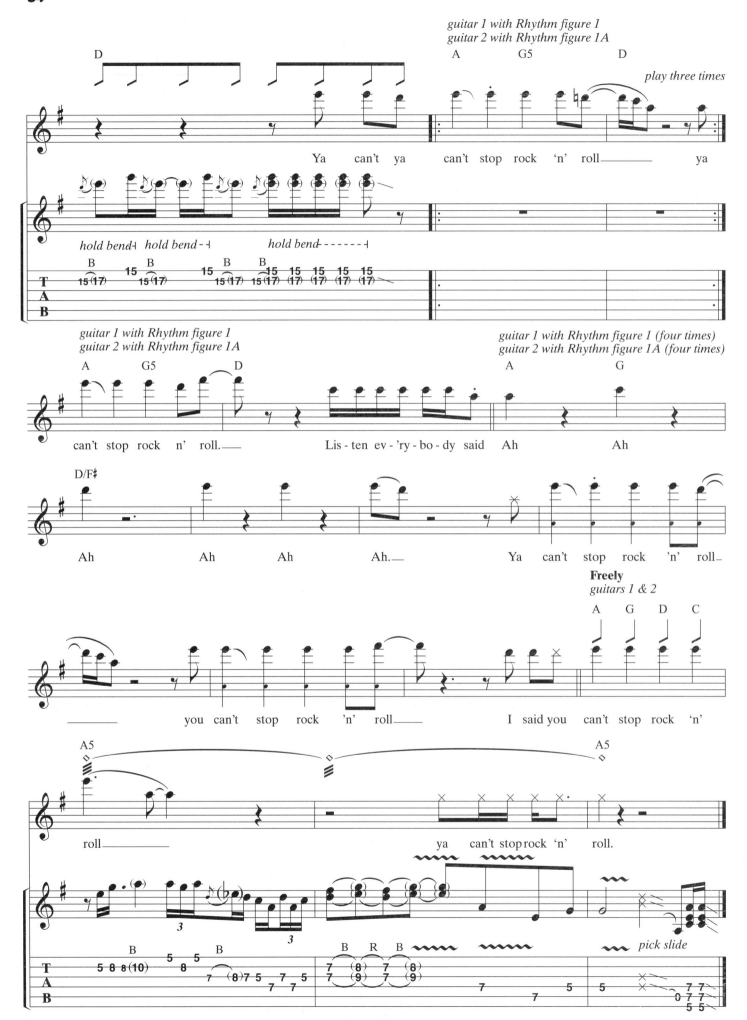

Damned

By Angus Young and Malcolm Young

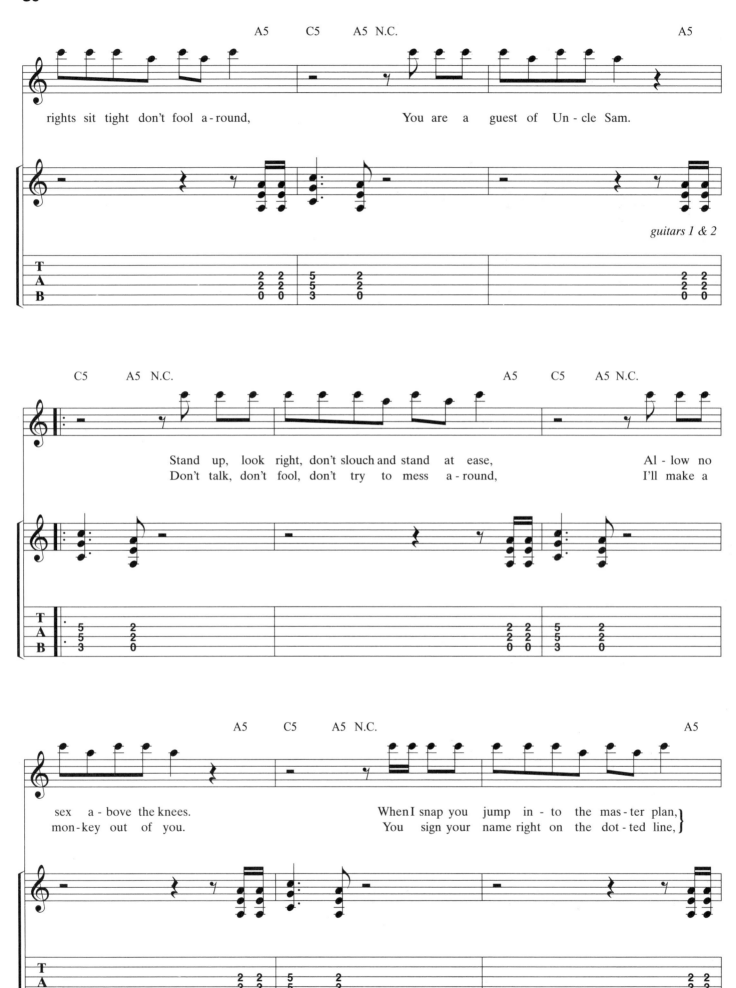

Satellite Blues

By Angus Young and Malcolm Young

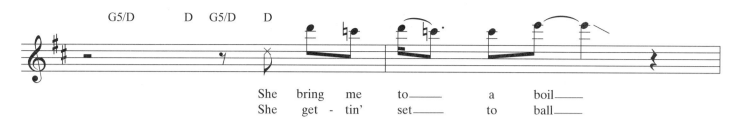

She   bring   me   to———   a   boil———
She   get - tin'   set———   to   ball———

She   like   to   give———   it   out   some
I   like   to   chew———   it   up   some

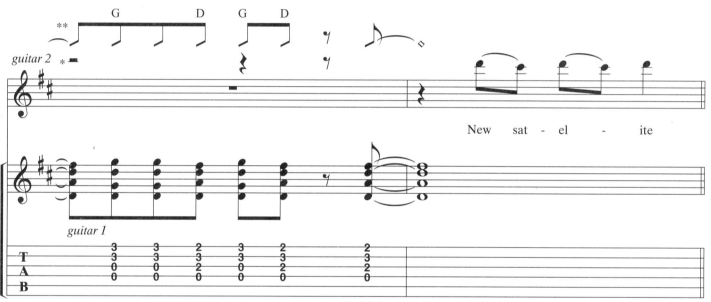

New   sat - el - ite

*first time ** second time

Chorus

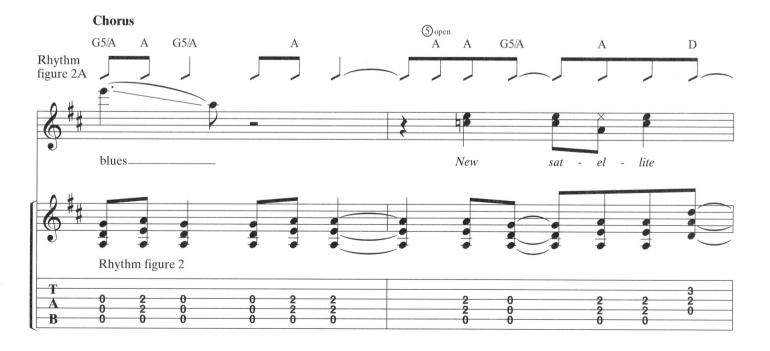

blues———

New   sat - el - lite

94

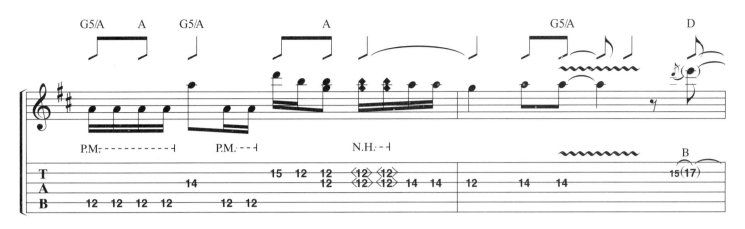

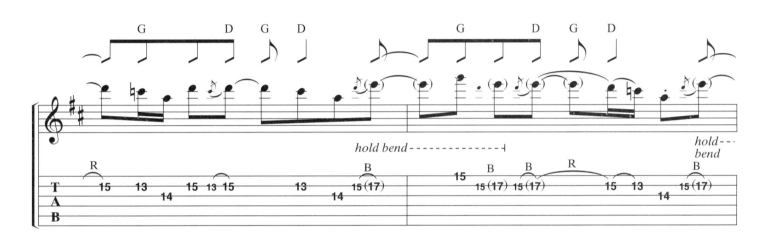

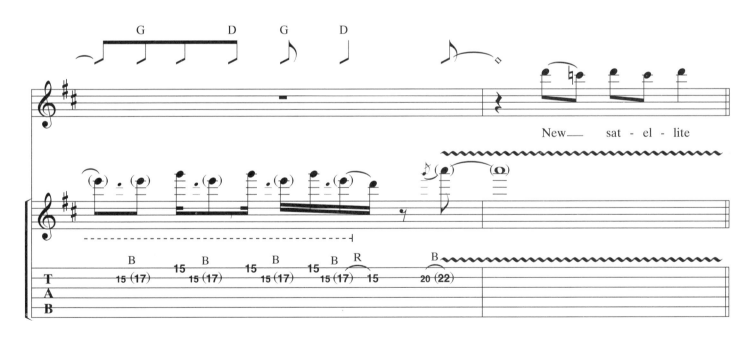

New — sat - el - lite

guitar 1 with Rhythm figure 2A (two times)
guitar 2 with Rhythm figure 3 (three and 3/4 times)

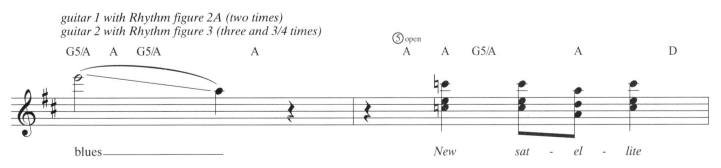

blues

New   sat - el - lite

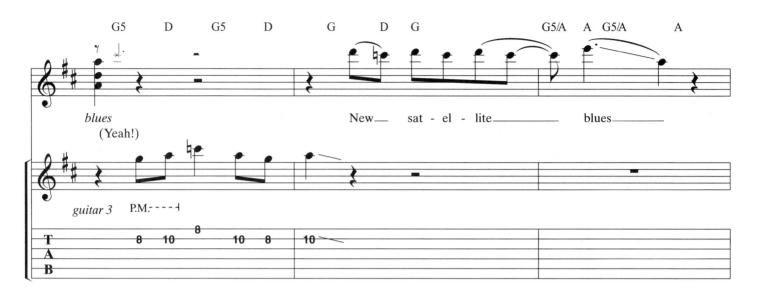

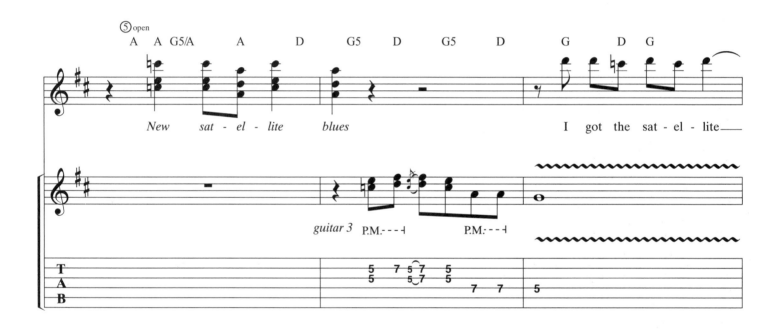

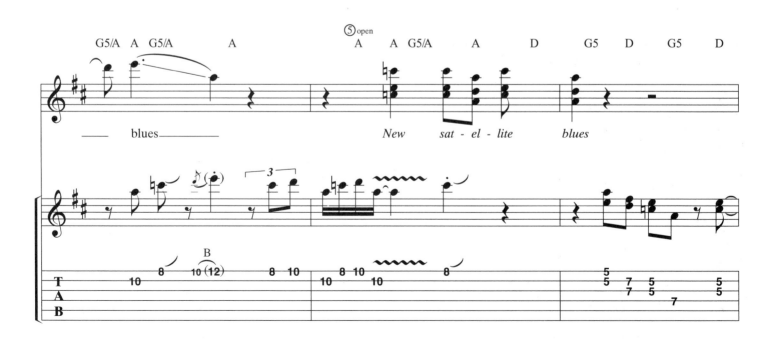

All Screwed Up
By Angus Young and Malcolm Young

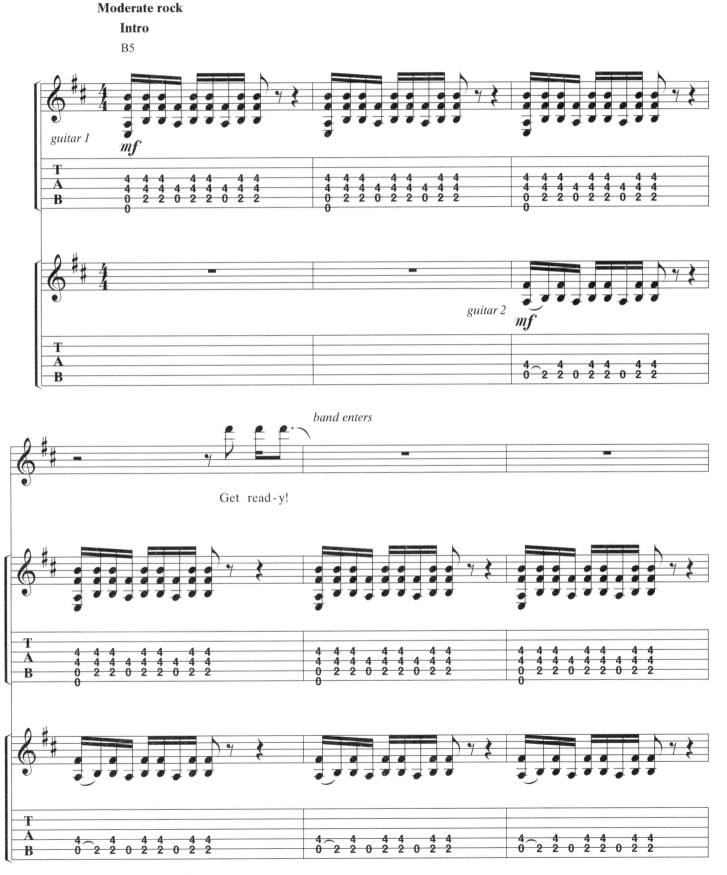

Verse

B5

1. You think you're kind - a
out to kick some-

tough._____ You walk____ kind - a rough._____ When
butt_____ work you o - ver screw you nuts_____ An' when

Chorus

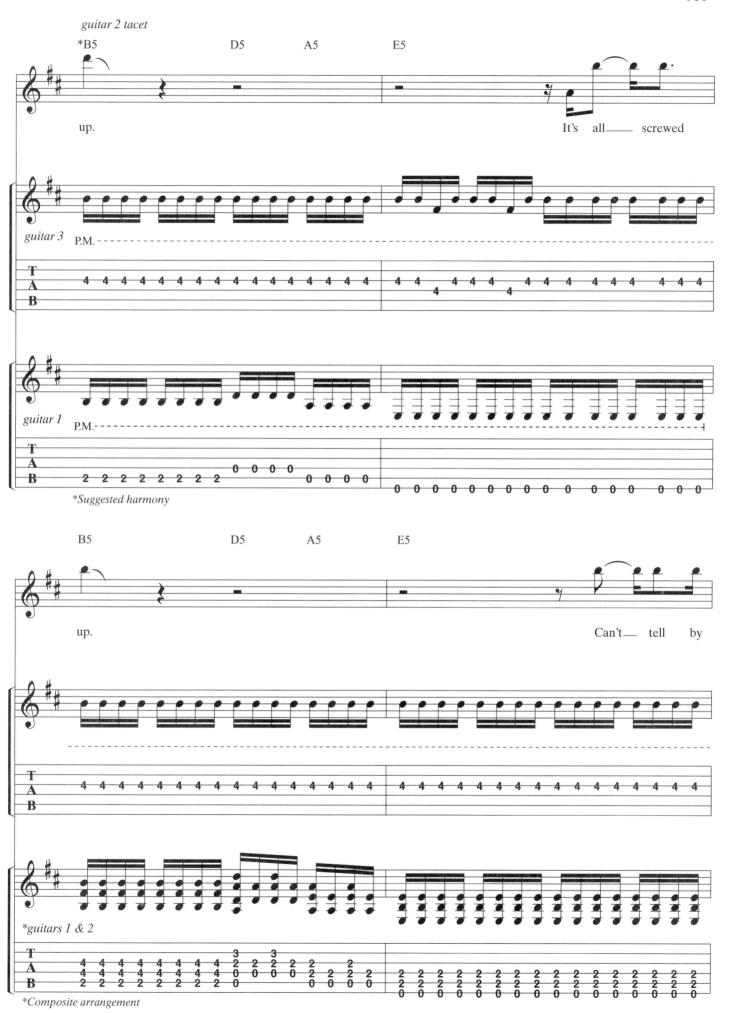

Guitar solo

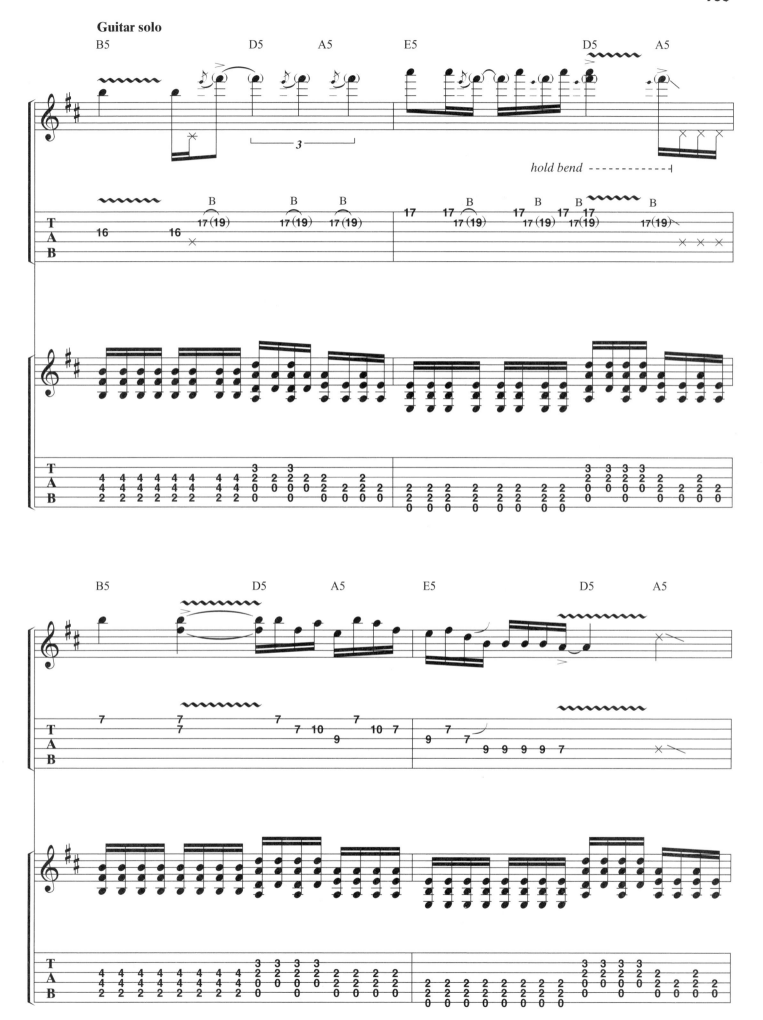

Chorus

I said you're all screwed— up.   All screwed

mp guitar 3

guitar 1 Rhythm figure 1

guitar 2 Rhythm figure 1A

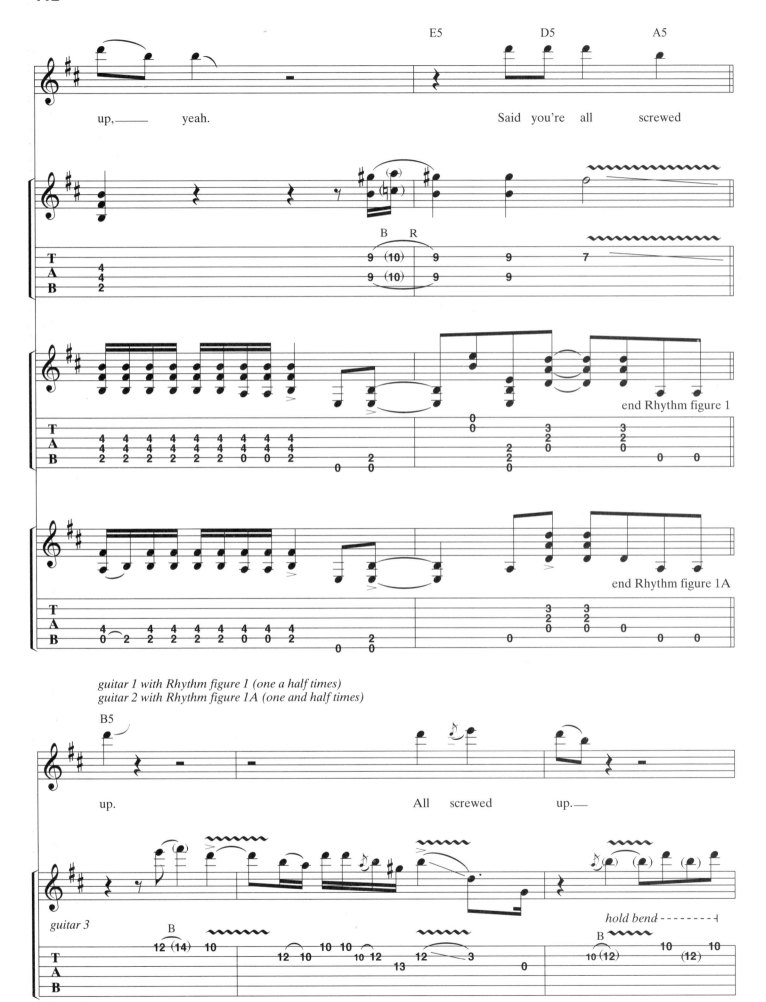

up,—— yeah.

Said you're all screwed

end Rhythm figure 1

end Rhythm figure 1A

guitar 1 with Rhythm figure 1 (one a half times)
guitar 2 with Rhythm figure 1A (one and half times)

up.

All screwed up.——

guitar 3

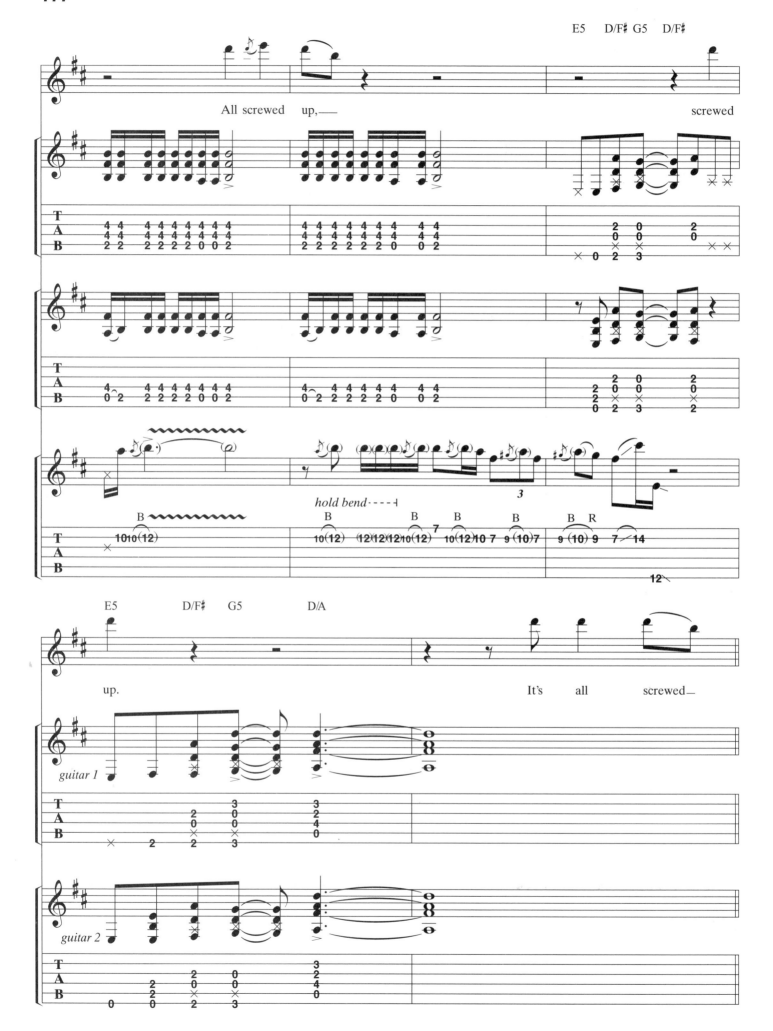

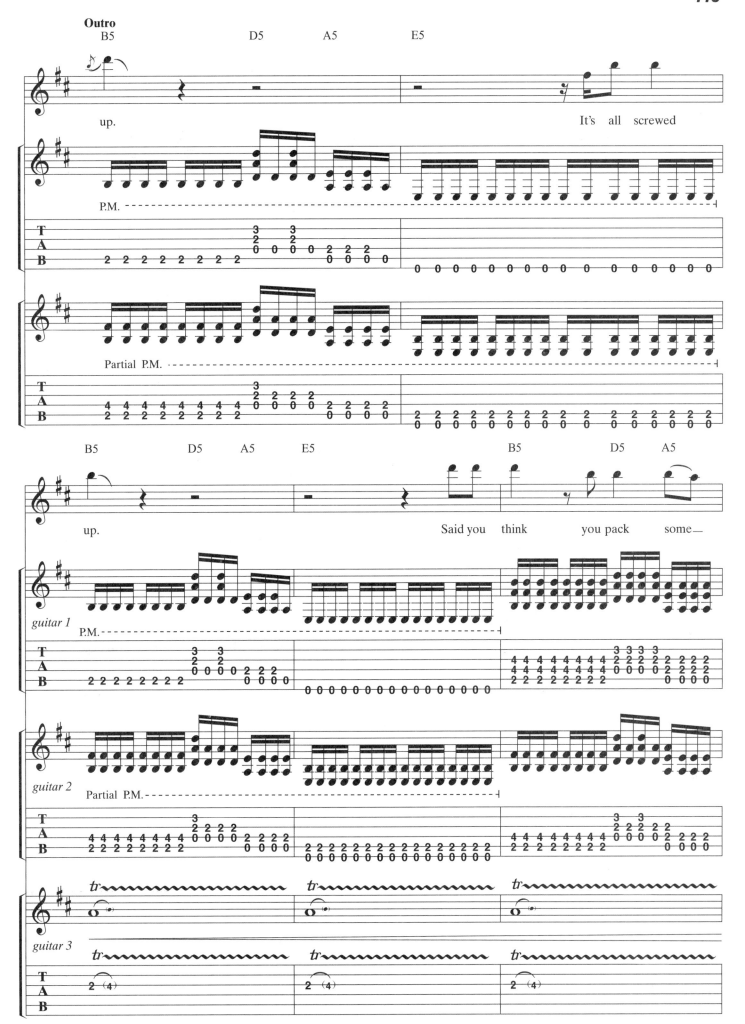

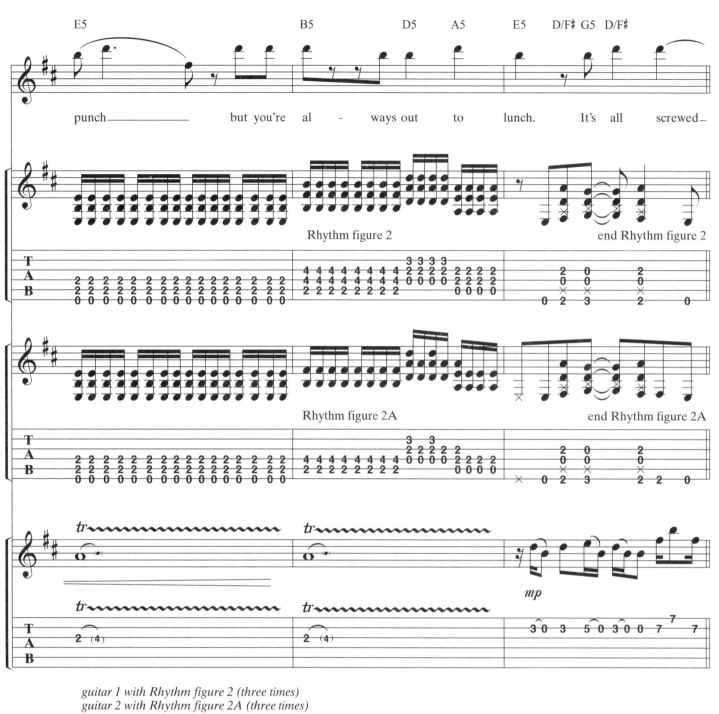

punch_____ but you're al - ways out to lunch. It's all screwed___

Rhythm figure 2

end Rhythm figure 2

Rhythm figure 2A

end Rhythm figure 2A

mp

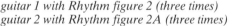

guitar 1 with Rhythm figure 2 (three times)
guitar 2 with Rhythm figure 2A (three times)

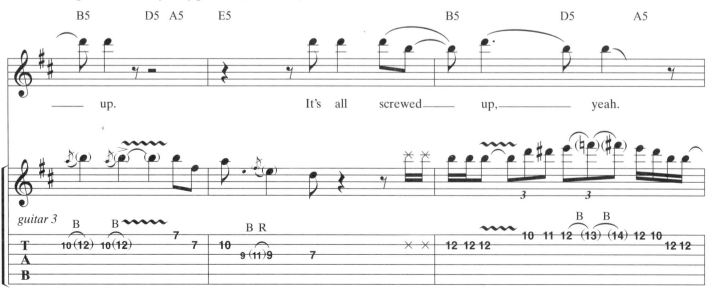

___ up. It's all screwed___ up,_____ yeah.

guitar 3

It's all screwed

Give It Up

By Angus Young and Malcolm Young

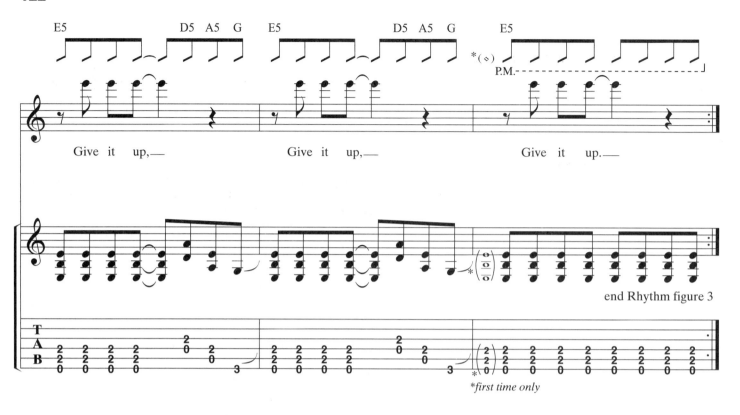

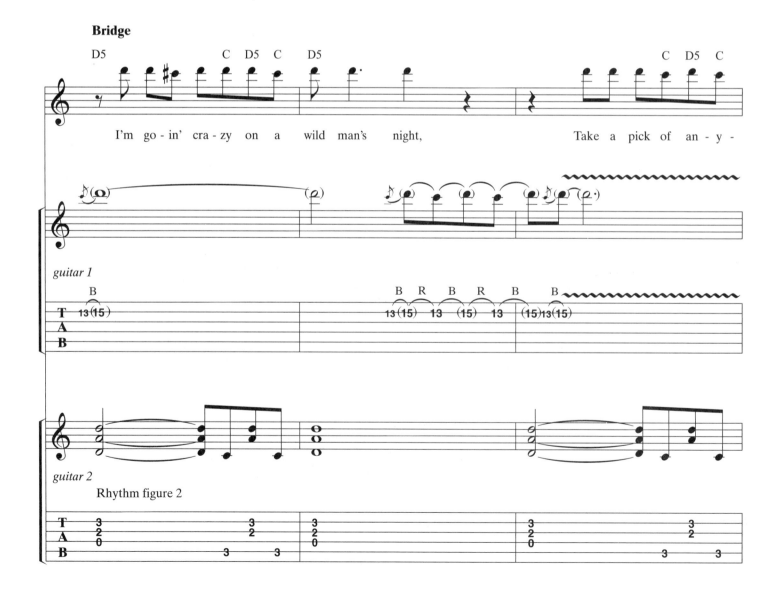

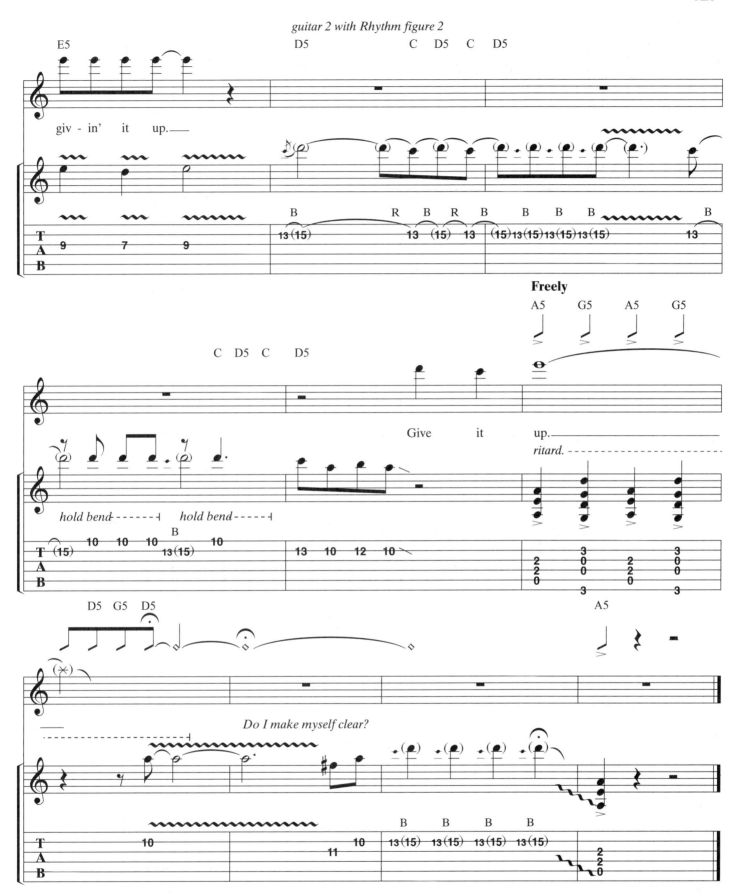

Additional lyrics

2. There's a big storm a howlin' around here.
There be no wine, no sinnin', and no beer.
Gonna aim to fire a rocket,
There ain't no damn way to stop it,
Got a sure fire bullet to get you outta here.
Do I make myself clear?
(to Pre-chorus)

Come and Get It

By Angus Young and Malcolm Young

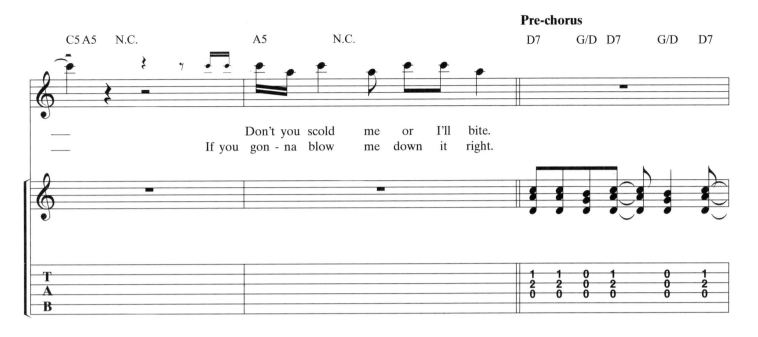

Don't you scold me or I'll bite.
If you gon - na blow me down it right.

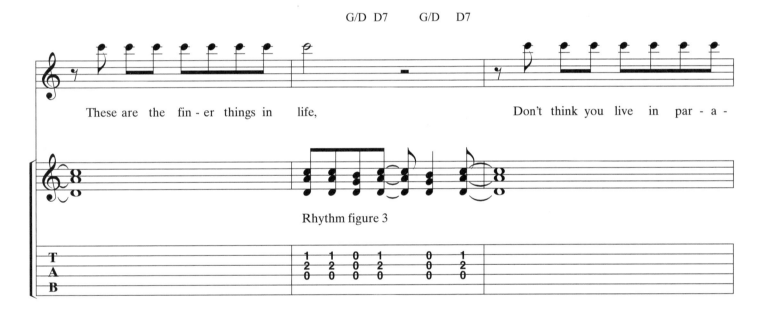

These are the fin - er things in life,

Don't think you live in par - a -

Rhythm figure 3

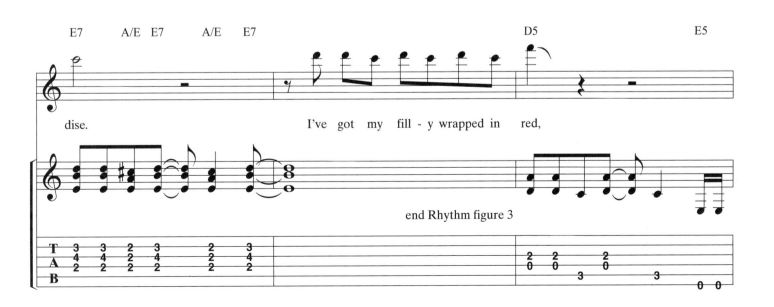

dise.

I've got my fill - y wrapped in red,

end Rhythm figure 3

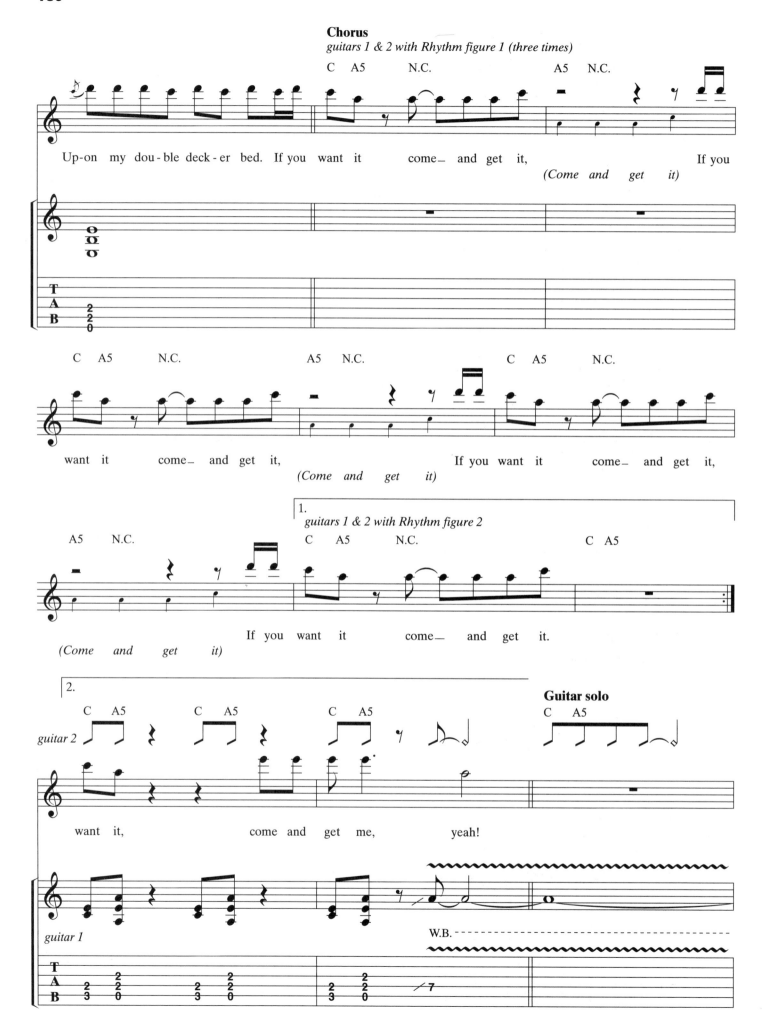

Come and get me!